S.D. OSSESSIONE

HER DARKEST DESIRES

A DARK ROMANCE GUIDE FOR MEN WHO DARE

First published by Dark Ossessione Press 2025

First edition

ISBN: 979-8-218-81999-6

This book was professionally typeset on Reedsy.
Find out more at reedsy.com

For the men bold enough to step into the shadows,
and for the women whose secret desires illuminate the way.
This book is dedicated to your courage, your passion,
and the love you dare to create together.

"To step into the darkness and return with her heart—that is the art of the Dark Romance Man."

S.D. Ossessione

Contents

Preface

This book was born from a simple question: *What do women really feel when they read dark romance, and how can men learn from it?*

For years, women have turned to these novels not just for entertainment, but for escape, exploration, and emotional charge. Between the shadows and the fire, they find something many men never realize they're missing in real-life intimacy: a combination of intensity, vulnerability, danger, and devotion.

As a man, I wanted to understand this world more deeply. What started as curiosity quickly became a mission. I discovered that dark romance novels are not merely fiction, but a coded language of desire. They show how women long to be pursued, claimed, challenged, and cherished. They also reveal how men can step into a more powerful role in their relationships—without losing tenderness or respect.

This book is not about copying fiction word for word, but about translating fantasy into reality. It is a guide for men who want to bridge the gap: to learn the emotional currents, the archetypes, the kinks, and the behaviors that make dark romance so magnetic to women.

My goal is simple: to give you insight and tools you can use to create richer intimacy with your partner. To help you become the kind of man who doesn't just exist in the pages of her favorite books, but in her real life.

If you read with an open mind—and an open heart—you'll see that this journey is not about pretending to be someone else. It is about becoming a fuller version of yourself: bold, aware, and willing to step into her shadows with confidence.

Continue your journey with other books in the **Her Darkest Desires** series. Each volume draws you further into the shadows of passion and power, where intimacy becomes daring, and desire transforms into obsession. Discover the thrill of whispered secrets, dangerous temptations, and unforgettable intimacy with every new book in the series.

S.D. Ossessione

Acknowledgments

Every book is born from more than one voice, and this one is no exception.

First, I want to thank the many **authors of dark romance** whose stories have ignited imaginations around the world. Their courage to write boldly about desire, danger, and intimacy created the foundation for this guide. Without their works, there would be no map for men to follow.

To the **women who read and shared their experiences**, thank you for your honesty. You opened the door to understanding what lies between the lines of these novels. Your willingness to talk about the feelings these books awaken has shaped every page of this work.

To the **men brave enough to ask questions and lean into discomfort**, you are proof that masculinity can be both strong and tender. You inspired me to create a resource that bridges the gap between fantasy and reality.

And to my closest circle — friends, confidants, and loved ones — your support made this book possible. You reminded me that even when writing about shadows, it is always love that lights the way.

Finally, to the readers holding this book now: thank you. By choosing to open these pages, you've chosen to explore a part of intimacy that is often hidden, whispered, or left in fiction. That choice alone makes you part of the story.

S.D. Ossessione

Prologue

INTO THE SHADOWS

You feel his presence before you see him. A shiver runs down your spine, not of fear, but of recognition. Somewhere in the dark, he is watching. Not waiting — watching. His focus is unshakable, as though nothing else in the world exists.

Your breath quickens. The room feels smaller, the night heavier. A door closes softly behind you, and you know without words that escape is impossible. And yet, you don't want to run.

When he steps from the shadows, there is no hesitation. His gaze pins you in place, fierce and unwavering. The world outside — with its noise, its obligations, its endless distractions — disappears. In this moment, there is only you and him.

He does not ask if you're ready. He knows you are. And when he speaks, his voice is low, certain, impossible to resist:
"You're mine now. And I won't let you go."

This is the fantasy women return to again and again. The danger that isn't danger. The surrender that feels like freedom. The darkness that transforms into desire.

This is not just fiction. This is the language of longing.

And if you, as a man, are willing to learn it — to step into her shadows and lead her back into the light — you will become more than the hero of her story. You will become the man she has always dreamed of.

Introduction

This is not a book about cliches, nor is it a manual of tired advice. This is a guide to one of the most overlooked truths about women's desires: the fantasies they explore through dark romance novels are not just idle entertainment — they are windows into what they long to feel in real life.

Women devour these books by the millions. They read them late at night, in secret, on lunch breaks, and in stolen moments. They laugh, cry, and ache with characters who are often nothing like the men they encounter day to day. And the question every man should be asking is: *why?*

The answer is layered. Dark romance stories are not simply tales of danger and love. They are coded messages. They are safe spaces for women to indulge in intensity, obsession, and surrender. They allow them to feel emotions that everyday life often dulls or dismisses. When a heroine is pursued relentlessly, protected fiercely, or cherished obsessively, women are not wishing for pain. They are longing for passion that feels unshakable.

As a man, this is your opportunity. You don't need to become a fictional antihero or pretend to be someone you're not. What you need is awareness. The ability to read between the lines and translate fantasy into reality. To understand that when she reads about surrender, she is longing for trust. When she thrills at danger, she is craving intensity. When she smiles at obsession, she is yearning to be chosen without hesitation.

This book will walk you through the essentials:

- Why women love dark romance, and what they gain from it.
- The desires and ideas these books awaken in them.
- The archetypes, attitudes, and behaviors of dark romance men.
- How to role play, experiment, and create scenarios that bring fantasy alive.
- How to balance passion with respect, safety, and consent.

Think of this book as both a mirror and a map. A mirror, because it reflects what women are already feeling when they read. A map, because it gives you practical tools to bring those feelings into your relationship.

You are not competing with her novels. You are learning from them. And if you read with the same focus that she reads her favorite stories, you will see: dark romance isn't a threat to real love. It is a gift, a guide, and a challenge to become the man she secretly dreams of.

CHAPTER 1 - UNDERSTANDING THE WORLD OF ROMANCE AND DARK ROMANCE

"Romance is the language of longing; dark romance is the dialect of desire unspoken"

Romance has long been the most beloved genre of fiction. For decades, it has outsold thrillers, mysteries, fantasy, and even science fiction combined. That alone tells us something powerful: love and the desire to feel deeply is universal. Yet, within this vast world of romance lies a sub genre that has exploded in popularity, especially among women: dark romance.

Unlike traditional romance, dark romance doesn't just focus on sweetness, happy coincidences, or lighthearted happily-ever-afters. It dares to dive into danger,obsession, power struggles, and the blurred lines between fear and desire. Its heroes are not flawless gentlemen or predictable "good guys." They are brooding,morally complex,even dangerous. And that is exactly why women cannot get enough of them.

Why Women Are Drawn to It

Women read dark romance because it offers what everyday life often withholds: intensity without real-world consequences. Between the covers of a book, they can experience obsession without harm, danger without actual threat, surrender without the loss of control.

Within fiction, they can immerse themselves in feelings that are both exhilarating and safe. A heroine may be stalked, claimed, or tempted by a forbidden figure, but the reader knows that she ultimately remains in control of the experience — she can close the book at any moment. That control creates safety, and safety makes even the darkest fantasies compelling.

What Sets Dark Romance Apart

Dark romance provides three unique ingredients that traditional romance often softens or avoids:

1. Heightened tension – Every glance, every touch, carries a charge of risk and desire.

2. Complex heroes – Men who terrify the world but protect the woman they love with ferocity.

3. Emotional extremes – Fear, surrender, passion, and transformation woven into a storm of feeling.

For men, this is the key takeaway: if women are devouring millions of these stories, it means they are craving more than politeness or predictability. They are craving intensity, attention, and devotion. The dark romance man is both danger and safety,dominance and loyalty. He frightens the world but treasures his heroine above all.

A Brief History

Fiction has always reflected cultural desires. In the 18th and 19th centuries, Gothic novels filled with haunted castles, secret passages, and brooding aristocrats became wildly popular among women. Those heroines were often trapped or imperiled — yet they were also pursued, desired, and transformed through love.

The archetype of the Gothic hero — mysterious, flawed, yet irresistible — is the direct ancestor of today's dark romance male lead. The difference? Modern dark romance makes the unspoken explicit. Where Gothic novels hinted at danger, today's dark romance immerses readers in it. Where classic romance promised tidy resolutions, dark romance revels in morally gray choices, obsession, and raw emotional intensity. With the rise of online communities, particularly BookTok and TikTok, dark romance has surged into mainstream culture. Women share quotes, fan art, and even dramatic re-enactments of their favorite scenes. Books like Haunting Adeline have become cult phenomena, showing just how deeply these stories resonate.

The Emotional Core

At its heart, dark romance is not about violence or cruelty. It is about emotional extremes. The thrill of being desired beyond reason. The fear of surrendering control. The sweetness of being protected after tension has built to its breaking point. Women are not just reading for plot — they are reading for immersion. They crave stories that make their hearts race, that leave them breathless, that awaken the most hidden corners of their imagination. Some of the key emotions dark romance stirs:

- Anticipation – The drawn-out, slow burn of pursuit.
- Fear & Thrill – The safety of danger experienced through fiction.
- Surrender & Trust – The release of control to someone both powerful and protective.
- Transformation – The heroine's personal growth through her relationship with a dangerous yet devoted man.

What This Means for Men

This chapter lays the foundation: to understand the appeal of dark romance is to understand women's hidden desires. The books are not blueprints to mimic, but they are signals. They reveal what women secretly crave: pursuit, intensity, and unwavering devotion.

The truth is, she doesn't want you to become a literal stalker, hit man, or mafia kingpin. What she wants is the feeling that these archetypes create. She wants to feel pursued as if she's the only woman in the world. She wants to feel safe in your arms but also excited by your intensity. She wants to surrender without fear, because she knows you'll never betray her trust.

Closing Thought

Dark romance is not a threat to love; it is a magnifier of it. These stories are a guide, an invitation, and a reminder. When you learn to see the world of dark romance as she does, you will discover what she secretly hopes you can provide. And you'll realize that stepping into her fantasies is not about pretending to be someone else — it's about showing her the depth of your passion, your attention, and your willingness to cherish her in ways that make her feel fully alive.

CHAPTER 2 - WHY WOMEN READ DARK ROMANCE

"The stories are not about monsters; they are about desire dressed in shadows."

A Deeper Look at Desire

When men first hear that women are devouring books about stalkers, villains, or morally gray antiheroes, the reaction is often confusion. "Why would she want to read about that?" The answer lies not in the literal scenarios but in the feelings those stories provoke.

Dark romance is not a guidebook for criminal behavior. It is an emotional laboratory, a place where women can test the boundaries of fear, desire, surrender, and intensity in a space that is completely safe. Between the pages of a book, she can feel pursued, claimed, or even endangered—yet she knows the danger is controlled. The moment she sets the book down, she is safe again.

The Power of Emotional Extremes

Think about why people watch horror movies. It's not because they want to be hunted by killers or chased through haunted houses. It's because the experience of fear—when contained—is exhilarating. The heart races, adrenaline surges, and the body comes alive.

For women, dark romance offers something even more intimate: the combination of fear and desire intertwined. A heroine may be trapped, stalked, or swept into forbidden encounters, but always with the promise of love at the core. The danger sharpens the desire, making the emotional payoff so much greater.

Mini Case Study – Haunting Adeline

A heroine feels a dangerous figure watching her, invading her world, claiming her as his obsession. Instead of retreating, she is drawn deeper into his intensity. Readers describe the experience as terrifying and irresistible at once — the thrill of being desired beyond reason.

Takeaway: It's not the act of stalking that appeals; it's the fantasy of being wanted so completely that nothing—not even moral boundaries—can stop it.

Safe Danger

This is the paradox at the heart of dark romance: women crave danger that is safe. A story allows them to surrender without consequence. They can feel the thrill of risk without being in real jeopardy. They can explore taboos without shame, because fiction is a private playground.

This is where many men misunderstand. They hear their partner rave about a book where a ruthless antihero locks a heroine in his mansion and think, "Do you want me to do that?" The answer is no. She doesn't want the literal situation. She wants the feeling that moment conveys: being chosen, being pursued, being unable to escape the pull of his desire.

Why Women Return to These Stories

1. Intensity Over Comfort – They already know what everyday comfort feels like. Dark romance gives them intensity.

2. Fantasy Without Consequence – They can experience taboo fantasies with zero real world risk.

3. The Ultimate Devotion – Even the most dangerous hero becomes tender and protective toward his heroine.

4. Emotional Release – Reading provides catharsis, an emotional storm that leaves them both shaken and satisfied.

Sidebar – Reader Voices

"I don't want a man to hurt me. But I want to know that he could — and that he never would."

"It's not the danger itself. It's the obsession behind it."

"Every woman wants to feel like she's the center of someone's universe. These books make me feel that way."

What Men Can Learn

When men dismiss dark romance as "unrealistic," they miss the point. Women aren't asking their partners to copy every plot line. They're asking them to recognize the desire beneath the fiction.

What she is really craving is:
- Pursuit – Show her that she is worth chasing.
- Obsession – Let her feel like she is at the center of your world.
- Intensity – Deliver emotions in bold strokes, not half-measures.
- Protection – Danger from the world, but safety in your arms.

Closing Thought

Dark romance thrives because it answers a question many women secretly carry: "Am I desirable enough to be pursued without end?" The books whisper back, "Yes."

As a man, your role is not to imitate the villains or antiheroes, but to understand what makes them compelling. When you learn to channel that energy into real life—through words, actions, and presence—you unlock something powerful. You step beyond the ordinary and into the realm where she feels both safe and breathlessly alive.

CHAPTER 3 - TOP 5 DARK ROMANCE BOOKS & WHAT THEY REVEAL

"Stories open the door to the fantasies she might never speak aloud."

Why Look at These Books?

To understand why women are drawn to dark romance, we need to examine the stories they are actually reading. These aren't niche or hidden titles. They are among the most popular books in the genre today, with millions of readers sharing them, recommending them on social media, and building communities around them.

By exploring what happens in these books — and how readers respond — men can uncover exactly what resonates with women. The key is not to imitate the literal actions of these fictional men, but to learn the emotional language behind the fantasy.

Haunting Adeline

Haunting Adeline by H.D. Carlton

Moment One – The Watching

Paraphrased: A heroine realizes she is being watched and followed by a dangerous man. His obsession is terrifying, yet she feels a pull instead of fear alone.

Synopsis: The violation of boundaries becomes the beginning of intimacy. His intensity transforms what should repel her into what fascinates her.

Reader Reaction: Fans say this is when they realized they were hooked — being wanted so completely was irresistible.

Takeaway for Men: Obsession translates to focus. Make her feel like she is the center of your attention.

Moment Two – The Claim
Paraphrased: He tells her, in his own way, that she belongs to him — not with gentle persuasion, but with dominance.

Synopsis: The act of possession flips from threatening to thrilling because she feels desired beyond reason.

Reader Reaction: Women describe goosebumps at the intensity, admitting they long to feel "claimed" without question in real life — safely.

Takeaway for Men: Claiming her in reality means loyalty and commitment, not control. Let her feel undeniably chosen.

Corrupt
Corrupt by Penelope Douglas

Moment One – The Masked Game

Paraphrased: The heroine enters a space where masked men blur danger and desire, and she realizes she is the focus of their attention.

Synopsis: The atmosphere of anonymity amplifies her fear and her arousal at once.

Reader Reaction: Readers call this scene unforgettable because of the heightened suspense.

Takeaway for Men: Mystery fuels desire. Use surprise and anticipation to keep passion alive.

Moment Two – The Confrontation

Paraphrased: The antihero corners the heroine, forcing her to confront the depth of his dominance.

Synopsis: It's raw, unsettling, and magnetic, pushing her to surrender not because she is weak but because he refuses to waver.

Reader Reaction: Fans describe being torn between fear and attraction, which makes the payoff more intense.

Takeaway for Men: Confidence is key. Don't confuse cruelty with conviction. Stand firm in pursuit, but keep her trust intact.

Credence

Credence by Penelope Douglas

Moment One – The Mountain Isolation

Paraphrased: The heroine finds herself surrounded by rugged men in an isolated cabin, where survival blurs into desire.

Synopsis: The isolation intensifies every glance and every touch.

Reader Reaction: Readers say the forbidden nature of the setup makes the story addictive.

Takeaway for Men: Boldness matters. In real life, embrace intensity and presence without apology.

Moment Two – The Taboo Tension

Paraphrased: The heroine experiences moments of temptation with men she shouldn't want. Desire collides with taboo.

Synopsis: The forbidden dynamic intensifies every interaction, creating explosive tension.

Reader Reaction: Women admit they couldn't look away — the shock factor was intoxicating.

Takeaway for Men: Taboo doesn't mean illegal. It means embracing what feels daring, new, and out of routine.

Butcher & Blackbird

Butcher & Blackbird by Brynne Weaver

Moment One – The First Hunt

Paraphrased: Two killers stalk each other, but the hunt becomes a game of desire.

Synopsis: Violence blurs into courtship, with danger fueling attraction.

Reader Reaction: Fans describe this as the most exhilarating introduction to a romance they'd ever read.

Takeaway for Men: Pursuit is thrilling. Show her she is worth chasing, worth your effort.

Moment Two – The Partnership
  Paraphrased: They reluctantly team up, turning from rivals into allies, and attraction burns beneath every move.

Synopsis: What began as enmity becomes intimacy, deepened by shared danger.

Reader Reaction: Readers loved the enemies-to-lovers progression, saying the chemistry was "explosive."

Takeaway for Men: Intimacy often begins with tension. Lean into playfulness and challenge — it can heighten desire.

Lights Out
  Lights Out by Navessa Allen

Moment One – The Capture
  Paraphrased: The heroine is forced into a situation where she must rely on a man whose danger is as evident as his strength.

Synopsis: Forced dependence becomes the foundation of trust.

Reader Reaction: Readers describe this as the moment they stopped breathing — fear giving way to safety.

Takeaway for Men: Trust is erotic. Be the man she can depend on when she feels most vulnerable.

Moment Two – The Confession

Paraphrased: Beneath his hard exterior, he admits his feelings in a moment of vulnerability.

Synopsis: The feared man reveals a softer truth, and the heroine realizes she is more than just protected — she is loved.

Reader Reaction: Women swoon at this shift from harshness to softness, calling it unforgettable.

Takeaway for Men: The sharpest contrast is power paired with vulnerability. Show both, and she will feel treasured.

Sidebar – Reader Voices

"I don't want to be kidnapped, but I want to be pursued. These books help me imagine that."

"When he turns from ruthless to tender, that's the moment I fall in love."

"The fantasy is about being desired beyond reason, not about being controlled."

Closing Thought

The most popular dark romance novels are not instruction manuals for bad behavior. They are emotional maps that reveal what women crave most: pursuit, intensity, protection, vulnerability, and devotion.

For men, the challenge is to step beyond everyday romance and deliver the essence — without ever crossing boundaries. Make her feel chosen, make her feel safe, and make her feel like her own private dark romance heroine.

Stories open the door to the fantasies she might never speak aloud. Your job is to listen, learn, and bring the essence to life.

CHAPTER 4 - THE DARK ROMANCE MALE ARCHETYPE

"He is both the storm and the shelter."

Why the Archetype Matters

If Chapter Two explored why women are drawn to dark romance, Chapter Four addresses who they are drawn to. The male figure in dark romance is not just a character — he is an archetype. He embodies a fusion of traits that seem contradictory: danger and devotion, cruelty and care, dominance and loyalty.

This archetype resonates because it taps into deep psychological and emotional currents. Women are not attracted to his crimes, violence, or flaws in themselves — they are attracted to the emotional experience he provides.

The Core Traits

1. Dominance Without Abandonment – He may command, control, or intimidate, but he never neglects. His dominance is paired with attentiveness.

2. Obsession With Devotion – He fixates on the heroine — not casually, not half halfheartedly. She becomes his axis, the one thing he cannot let go of.

3. Dark Power Coupled With Protection – To the world, he may be feared. To her, he is the safest place she knows.

4. Moral Ambiguity, Emotional Clarity – He breaks laws, crosses lines, and thrives in the gray— but his love for her is absolute.

Mini Case Study – Corrupt (paraphrased)

The antihero is dangerous, vengeful, and morally gray. Yet, when it comes to the heroine, his focus shifts. His obsession manifests as protection, passion, and complete fixation. Readers describe feeling simultaneously afraid of him and comforted by him.

Takeaway: The thrill lies in knowing that all of his ferocity is directed at the world, while his tenderness is reserved for her.

The Archetype Through Time

This figure is not new. Gothic literature gave us the brooding aristocrat in his castle. Victorian novels gave us the tortured Byronic hero. Today's dark romance amplifies him into mafia dons, stalkers, assassins, and morally gray billionaires. Across time, one thing is constant: the heroine transforms the dangerous man. He may never become lawful or "good" in society's terms, but he becomes safe and tender for her.

Sidebar – Reader Voices

"I don't want a nice guy. I want a dangerous man who is only gentle with me."

"The darker he is to the world, the more intoxicating it is when he is soft with her."

"It's about being chosen above everything else — even his own morality."

Why Men Should Pay Attention

The archetype teaches men that power, intensity, and devotion are not contradictions. A man can be firm, passionate, and even intimidating in his presence while also being gentle, safe, and loyal to his partner.

Key lessons for men:
- Be decisive. Indecision kills attraction.
- Show unwavering focus. Make her feel like she is the center of your universe.
- Channel strength into safety. Let her feel the power of your presence, but only as her protector.
- Don't dilute intensity. Politeness is fine; passion is unforgettable.

Closing Thought

The dark romance archetype endures because it embodies what many women secretly crave: a man who frightens the world but treasures his woman.

As a man, you don't need to mimic villains or criminals to step into this role. What matters is adopting the essence: unwavering devotion, bold intensity, and the ability to make her feel like the most desired, most protected person in existence.

He is both the storm that rattles the world and the shelter she runs into when it breaks.

CHAPTER 5 - ARCHETYPES OF THE DARK ROMANCE MAN

"Every shadow wears a different mask."

Why Archetypes Matter

The male figures in dark romance are not one-size-fits-all. Each archetype represents a different shade of darkness, a different fantasy of power and passion. While Chapter Four explored the single archetype as a concept, this chapter breaks down the major categories of men in dark romance fiction — what they embody, why women are drawn to them, and how men in real life can translate those elements into relationship dynamics.

Understanding these archetypes helps men see that dark romance isn't only about a "bad boy" stereotype. It's a tapestry of variations, each one fulfilling different emotional needs and desires.

Archetype One

The Obsessive Protector

He watches. He waits. He doesn't let her go. His obsession borders on unhealthy in the narrative, yet it translates into a feeling of being profoundly chosen.

Appeal to Women: She feels desired beyond reason. His devotion never wavers.

Lesson for Men: In real life, obsession doesn't mean control — it means attentiveness. Show her she matters through focus and unwavering presence.

Mini Case Study: In Haunting Adeline, the male lead's intensity is dangerous on paper, but the fantasy of being someone's undeniable focus is what grips readers.

Archetype Two
The Powerful Kingpin

Mafia bosses, criminal masterminds, ruthless billionaires — these figures command empires. Their power is dangerous, but their heroine is the one person who softens them.

Appeal to Women: The fantasy of security, luxury, and protection in exchange for surrender.

Lesson for Men: Real-world takeaway isn't money or crime; it's leadership. Women admire decisiveness and confidence.

Reader Voice: "I don't need a mob boss in my life, but I want to feel like my partner can take control when life gets hard."

Archetype Three
  The Tortured Byronic Hero

This is the man haunted by his own demons. He is brooding, wounded, and emotionally unavailable — until her presence cracks him open.

Appeal to Women: The trans-formative power of love. She becomes the only one who can reach him.

Lesson for Men: Vulnerability is strength. Sharing your struggles and letting her in deepens intimacy.

Mini Case Study: In Credence, the complex male figures are rugged, broken, and at times unapproachable — yet readers are drawn to the moments of vulnerability.

Archetype Four
  The Ruthless Villain Redeemed

This is the man who begins as an enemy, captor, or outright villain. But over time, his brutality shifts into protection, and his heart is revealed.

Appeal to Women: The thrill of danger combined with the fantasy of being the one who changes him.

Lesson for Men: Redemption doesn't mean you need to be "bad" first. It means showing growth, admitting flaws, and changing for her.

Archetype Five

The Playful Predator

This archetype blends darkness with charm. He teases, mocks, and seduces, but always with a razor's edge beneath his smile.

Appeal to Women: Danger laced with wit — he keeps her on edge in multiple ways.

Lesson for Men: Use humor and play as part of passion, but pair it with seriousness when it matters.

Sidebar – Consent Across Archetype

Regardless of the archetype, what makes them alluring in fiction is the safety net underneath. Women know these men, however dark, will not betray the heroine's trust. In real life, a man must prioritize communication, respect, and the ability to read her cues.

"The fantasy is that he could destroy the world — but never me."

Closing Thought

These archetypes may seem like fantasy extremes, but each contains a kernel of truth that men can embody. You don't need to become a mafia boss, stalker, or assassin.

What you can do is learn:

From the Obsessive Protector: pay attention.

From the Powerful Kingpin: lead with confidence.

From the Tortured Hero: let her in.

From the Redeemed Villain: show growth and devotion.

From the Playful Predator: use charm and playfulness to heighten passion.

The archetypes of the dark romance man are mirrors of desire. Each one reveals what women crave: intensity, devotion, transformation, leadership, and passion.

The man who understands these archetypes doesn't have to pick just one mask. He can weave them together into a dynamic, unforgettable presence — her personal dark romance hero in real life.

Every shadow wears a different mask. The question is: which one will you choose to wear for her?

CHAPTER 6 - MASKS, SYMBOLS, AND FANTASIES UNVEILED

"Every mask conceals, but it also reveals what we long to hide."

Why Symbols Matter Dark romance lives and breathes through symbols. A mask, a locked door, a set of cuffs, a ritual candle — these aren't props, they're portals into heightened emotion. Women respond to these images because they magnify vulnerability, mystery, and surrender.

The truth is: symbols work because they allow us to act out fantasies in ways that feel safer, more dramatic, and more intense. When done correctly, these fetishes are not only arousing, but they can actually increase closeness and pleasure between partners.

The Mask

In Fiction: Masks make heroines step into mystery — whether it's a masquerade in Corrupt or the chilling presence in Haunting Adeline. They create anticipation by hiding identity and intensifying uncertainty.

Why It Excites: The hidden face strips away control. Desire rises when other senses are heightened — she's forced to feel rather than anticipate.

Do It Right: Use a satin mask or even a blindfold. Make it comfortable, not suffocating. Let her know what you plan to do so she can lean into suspense without fear.

Increases Pleasure: Sensory play - when she can't see, every touch, whisper, or kiss feels amplified. Anticipation itself becomes foreplay.

Restraints - Chains, Ropes, and Restraints

In Fiction: Symbolize surrender and control. A heroine tied or pinned mirrors the fantasy of "losing power" while knowing she is secretly safe.

Why It Excites: Restriction removes choice in the moment, which magnifies sensation. She isn't deciding — she's simply feeling.

Do It Right: Always discuss first. Start small: silk scarves, soft restraints, or light pressure with your hands. Use safe words or signals. Avoid tight knots or anything that risks circulation.

Increases Pleasure: Restraints focus attention on the areas you touch. When she can't move, even a light stroke or kiss feels magnified, flooding her with sensation.

Bruises - Blood, Bruises, and Darkness

In Fiction: These darker visuals show passion so fierce it leaves a mark. In Butcher & Blackbird, bruises symbolize intimacy through extremity.

Why It Excites: Fictional bruises symbolize being "wanted too much." It's a fantasy of being consumed.

Do It Right: Marks should always be playful, not harmful. Light biting, sucking, or scratching can leave temporary marks without pain. Keep it within her comfort zone.

Increases Pleasure: Slight pain can sharpen pleasure — it releases endorphins, making the moment more intense. When framed as devotion, it deepens the feeling of being passionately claimed.

Shadows - Shadows and Secrecy

In Fiction: Hidden meetings, dangerous secrets, and nighttime encounters build irresistible suspense. In Lights Out, secrecy drives the erotic charge.

Why It Excites: Secrets feel intimate. The act of "what if we're discovered?" adds adrenaline to desire.

Do It Right: Create private rituals — surprise her with a whispered plan, role play secrecy in public (a hidden touch under the table), or keep playful secrets between you two.

Increases Pleasure: The thrill of secrecy releases adrenaline, which amplifies arousal. It turns the mundane into something electric.

Rituals - Rituals and Dark Romance Aesthetics

In Fiction: Gothic mansions, candlelight, blood oaths — rituals heighten the atmosphere. They give intimacy a stage.

Why It Excites: Rituals make sex feel more sacred, dramatic, and meaningful. They create anticipation and immersion.

Do It Right: It can be as simple as lighting candles, using a certain song, or whispering the same words at the moment of climax. The point is repetition that becomes your own shared language.

Increases Pleasure: Rituals build mental arousal before physical touch even begins. By the time you reach her, she's already immersed in the scene you've created together.

Sidebar – The Psychology of Fetishes

Fetishes are exaggerations of ordinary desires. They stretch emotions until they become theatrical. A blindfold stretches mystery. A restraint stretches surrender. A ritual stretches intimacy.

When handled safely and with consent, fetishes unlock heightened pleasure because they bypass the rational mind and activate raw, instinctual responses.

The key: consent, communication, and aftercare. Without those, the magic collapses.

Reader Voices

"Blindfold me and I'll feel every kiss a hundred times more."

"Restraints make me let go — my mind finally shuts off."

"A candlelit ritual before sex makes it feel like something sacred."

Closing Thought

Masks, chains, shadows, rituals — they aren't instructions for bad behavior. They're shortcuts into heightened intimacy. When men understand the psychology of these symbols and apply them with respect, they can take an ordinary encounter and turn it into something unforgettable.

Done correctly, fetishes don't just increase arousal — they increase connection, intimacy, and pleasure.

Every mask conceals, but it also reveals what we long to hide.

CHAPTER 7 – FANTASY AND ROLE PLAY

"Fantasy is the bridge between her imagination and your reality."

Why Fantasy Matters

Women read dark romance because it allows them to live out fantasies that feel too risky, taboo, or unrealistic to speak out loud. Role play and fantasy aren't about pretending to be someone you're not — they're about giving permission for imagination to become intimacy.

For men, learning to engage in fantasy means you stop competing with the characters in her books and start embodying the essence of what excites her.

Core

The Core of Fantasy

In Fiction: Dark romance heroines fall into scenarios they can't control: stalked, captured, seduced, dominated. These aren't literal instructions — they're symbolic representations of deep desire.

Why It Excites: Women get to feel unsafe while knowing they are safe. Fantasy is safe danger.

Do It Right: Talk openly before role play. Ask: "Do you want to try a scenario where you're the innocent and I'm the dangerous one?" Her answer sets the rules.

Increases Pleasure: Fantasy suspends the ordinary. A bedroom can feel like a castle, a prison, or a secret hideaway — and her arousal grows with the story you create together.

Scenarios

Role Play Scenarios in Dark Romance

Here are some of the most popular fantasy themes, with safe ways to translate them:

The Captive and the Keeper
In Fiction: The heroine is trapped, dependent on the
dark hero.
In Real Life: Recreate by taking control of the environment - guiding her movements,
speaking firmly, or lightly restraining her.
Pleasure Boost: Gives her permission to surrender fully, amplifying her arousal.

The Masquerade Encounter
In Fiction: Mystery fuels desire — she doesn't know who holds her.
In Real Life: Use masks, dim lighting, or a blindfold. Whisper instead of speaking
normally.

Pleasure Boost: Heightens anticipation. Every touch becomes electric when her vision is blocked.

The Forbidden Teacher / Protector

In Fiction: Authority meets vulnerability.

In Real Life: Role play as the confident guide, instructing her what to do, praising or

commanding.

Pleasure Boost: Power exchange sharpens her sense of being wanted and guided.

Dialogue

Scripted Words and Dialogue

In dark romance, dialogue is just as powerful as action. Men can learn to use phrases that carry weight:

"You're mine tonight."

"Don't move until I tell you."

"I'm watching you."

Why It Works: These words place her in the world of fantasy, signaling dominance, desire, and intensity.

Do It Right: Keep dialogue consensual. Ask beforehand what words excite her and which don't.

Safety

Boundaries and Safety

Role play is only powerful if safety is intact. Women can only surrender if they feel sure they won't be pushed beyond what they agreed.

- Set a Safe Word: Something neutral like "red" or "enough" ensures she can stop the scene instantly.
- Check In: Read her breathing, body language, and tone — sometimes her body will tell you more than her words.
- Aftercare: Once the fantasy ends, step back into tenderness. Hold her, reassure her, and remind her she is safe and adored.

Sidebar – The Brain on Fantasy

Studies show that the brain processes fantasy role play almost like reality. Adrenaline and dopamine spike, which can make orgasms more powerful and intimacy more lasting. That's why acting out fantasies can be so much more impact than routine sex — it taps into primal neurological responses.

Reader Voices

"When he whispered, 'Don't move,' I swear I stopped breathing. It wasn't about control — it was about surrender."

"I love the idea of being the captive because it lets me shut off my mind. He takes over, and I just feel."

"Role play makes me feel like I'm living inside the book. It's intoxicating."

Closing Thought

Fantasy isn't lying. It isn't pretending. It's giving yourself and your partner permission to explore, exaggerate, and escape.

In dark romance, heroines fall for men who can create worlds of passion, fear, and devotion. In reality, your power lies not in being dangerous, but in crafting safe danger — the thrill without the threat, the surrender without the fear, the fantasy with the guarantee of intimacy and love.

Fantasy is the bridge between her imagination and your reality. Cross it with her, and you'll discover desire she didn't know how to ask for.

CHAPTER 8 - FETISHES AND KINKS

"Kink is not chaos — it is desire structured with care."

Why Kinks Matter

Kinks and fetishes are the heartbeat of dark romance fiction. They push boundaries, heighten intensity, and transform ordinary intimacy into something unforgettable. In novels, they appear heightened and theatrical. In reality, they require careful handling — but when done right, they can unlock deeper pleasure and intimacy.

Understanding

Understanding Kink

- In Fiction: A heroine is pushed into scenarios involving dominance, restraints, or other unconventional practices.
- Why It Excites: The thrill comes not from danger itself, but from the emotional charge surrender, loss of control, or taboo pleasure.
- In Real Life: Kink is an agreement. Both partners step into a world where roles, limits, and expectations are clear. Guiding Principle: Kink without consent is abuse. Kink with communication is erotic theater.

Popular

Popular Kinks in Dark Romance (and Safe Translations)

Dominance and Submission

- In Fiction: The male lead exerts power; the heroine submits.
- In Real Life: Power exchange is agreed upon. He takes the lead, she agrees to follow.
- Safe Translation: Clear boundaries, verbal agreements, and aftercare.
- Pleasure Boost: Submissive often report that surrendering gives them release from stress, heightening physical pleasure.

Roughness (Hair-Pulling, Spanking, Gripping)

- In Fiction: Roughness is a sign of intensity and passion.
- In Real Life: Needs communication on intensity. Start light, watch reactions.
- Safe Translation: Open dialogue: "Harder or softer?"
- Pleasure Boost: Sharp sensations trigger adrenaline and endorphins, amplifying orgasms.

Role Reversals

- In Fiction: Sometimes the heroine surprises by seizing control.
- In Real Life: Men can allow their partner to dominate or command.
- Safe Translation: Switch roles intentionally — let her lead the scene.
- Pleasure Boost: Experiencing both roles deepens empathy and intimacy.

Exhibitionism and Secrecy

- In Fiction: Encounters in risky or semi-public settings.
- In Real Life: Risk should be symbolic, not illegal. Try dim lights, open windows, or "almost caught" scenarios.
- Pleasure Boost: Adrenaline sharpens arousal and strengthens bonding.

Safety

The Golden Rule: Safety and Consent

Every kink should follow three principles:

- Safe: No risk of physical harm beyond what's agreed.
- Sane: Both partners remain emotionally grounded.
- Consensual: Clear "yes" before play begins.

Communication

Communication Tips for Exploring Kink

- Start with Curiosity: "What excites you when you read these books?"
- Offer Options: "Would you like me to take full control, or just guide?"
- Set a Safe Word: Neutral, easy to remember.
- Debrief Afterward: Ask her what she enjoyed most and what could be improved.

Sidebar – The Power of Anticipation

Anticipation is one of the strongest aphrodisiacs. Talking about a kink days in advance, hinting at what will happen, or sending her a teasing message primes her arousal before the moment begins. Dark romance thrives on this — building slow, delicious dread before the climax.

Reader Voices

"I love when he pulls my hair because it feels raw, but I need to know he's still gentle underneath."

"My favorite part of kink is the moment right before — when I know something is coming but I don't know exactly what."

"We tried role play with a safe word. Just knowing I could stop it made me feel free to let go completely."

Closing Thought

Kinks and fetishes are not about deviancy. They are tools for intimacy. Done correctly, they create spaces where women can feel consumed, cherished, and thrilled all at once.

The man who explores kink with care, respect, and boldness will not only heighten pleasure but deepen trust. He will give her what she craves from her dark romance novels — a fantasy made safe, thrilling, and real.

Kink is not chaos — it is desire structured with care.

CHAPTER 9 - INTIMACY AND EMOTIONAL DEPTH

"The deepest passion is born where vulnerability meets devotion."

Introduction: Why Emotional Depth Matters in Dark Roman

Dark romance novels draw their power not only from their danger, mystery, or forbidden themes, but also from their undercurrent of intimacy and emotional depth. Women do not fall in love with the hero simply because he is commanding or ruthless; they fall in love because beneath that surface, he is consumed with desire, loyal in ways no one else dares to be, and deeply attuned to the woman he chooses. The blend of darkness with devotion, of dominance with vulnerability, creates the spellbinding tension that keeps readers hooked.

For men seeking to bring dark romance into real relationships, this is the crucial lesson: emotional intimacy is not optional—it is the foundation that makes the fantasy work. The moments of daring, control, or intensity are thrilling only because they exist inside a container of trust and connection. When a woman allows herself to surrender to a fantasy, it is because she knows—consciously or subconsciously—that the man she is with cherishes her completely. Intimacy is the tether that turns shadows into sanctuary.

The Hidden Longing for Connection Beneath the Fantasy

On the surface, dark romance stories can look like they are about danger, power struggles, or even obsession. But what makes them irresistible is the promise of connection beneath the chaos. A heroine might be swept into a risky situation or tested by a dominant partner, yet the true fantasy is not danger for its own sake—it is the thrill of being chosen, protected, and fully claimed by someone who sees her in ways no one else does.

Women crave not only the boldness of the hero, but also the hidden tenderness beneath his armor. His willingness to risk everything for her, his fierce loyalty, his relentless focus—these are the emotional payoffs that balance the danger. It is this fusion of power with devotion that makes dark romance resonate so deeply.

Men often underestimate how powerful emotional grounding can be in fueling desire. They may assume that strength alone wins a woman's heart. In truth, strength without intimacy feels hollow, like a performance. But strength coupled with emotional depth—genuine listening, real presence, the courage to be vulnerable—becomes

irresistible. It allows a woman to feel safe enough to explore the edges of fantasy. In this way, emotional intimacy is not a softening of masculinity, but its sharpening. It is what transforms intensity into connection.

When Emotion Meets Physical Intimacy

In dark romance novels, physical encounters are never just about the body. They are charged with meaning because of the emotions swirling beneath the surface—longing, devotion, obsession, and trust. A commanding touch feels electric not because of the act itself, but because the heroine knows it carries layers of intent: I see you. I want you. I will never let you go.

In real life, this is where men often miss the mark. Physical intimacy without emotional connection can feel routine, even empty. But when emotion is woven in—when each touch is anchored in care, when eye contact carries devotion, when words are spoken with intensity—the experience deepens. Emotional closeness heightens physical desire, and physical closeness reinforces emotional intimacy. Together, they create a feedback loop that strengthens the bond.

For couples who want to bring dark romance to life, emotional intimacy becomes the invisible safety net. It allows for more daring play, for bolder expressions of dominance or fantasy. Without emotional depth, those same actions might feel frightening or alienating. With emotional depth, they feel exhilarating. The difference is trust. She can embrace intensity precisely because she knows that beneath it lies unwavering care.

Vulnerability: The Strength Behind the Mask

At first glance, the dark romance hero seems invulnerable. He commands, controls,and protects with unshakable confidence. Yet what makes him truly captivating is the rare glimpse of vulnerability— the crack in the armor that reveals his raw desire, his fear of losing her, his secret longing for closeness. That juxtaposition of power and vulnerability is what makes the relationship unforgettable.

Men in real life often shy away from vulnerability, believing it undermines authority or strength. But the opposite is true. Vulnerability, when expressed with authenticity, demonstrates courage. It says: I trust you enough to show you who I really am. In a relationship framed by dark romance, vulnerability is what prevents dominance from feeling cold or distant. It infuses intensity with humanity.

Imagine telling your partner not only that you desire her, but that you need her—that she is the one who disarms you, who can reach you in ways no one else can. This is not weakness; it is devotion. In fact, the dark romance archetype thrives on obsession and passion

45

precisely because vulnerability pulses beneath the surface. When a man allows glimpses of his inner world—his fears, his hopes, his tenderness— he becomes more than a commanding presence. He becomes a safe, consuming force of connection.

Being Present and Attuned in Fantasy

Presence is one of the most overlooked, yet most powerful, qualities a man can bring to intimacy. In a dark romance scene, the heroine always feels seen. The hero does not fumble distractedly or act without awareness—he is utterly focused on her. His gaze is unwavering, his timing precise, his attention complete. She feels like the center of his universe, and that intensity amplifies everything.

Real intimacy works the same way. When you are present—silencing distractions, focusing fully on your partner—you communicate something profound: You matter. I am here with you, fully. Presence transforms even ordinary moments into something electric. A kiss becomes more than a kiss; a touch becomes more than a touch.

Attunement takes this presence a step further. It means reading cues, adjusting pace,and responding to subtle signals. In dark romance fantasies, this attunement is essential: the heroine pushes boundaries only because she senses that the hero is attuned enough to catch her if she falters. In real life, being attuned to your partner's body language, expressions, and words is what keeps fantasy safe and thrilling. It ensures that intensity never tips into discomfort, and that closeness always remains anchored in care.

Building Trust Through Intensity

Trust is the foundation upon which every dark romance story is built. A woman surrenders to danger, obsession, or dominance not because she is naive, but because she trusts the man behind the intensity. She knows, instinctively, that he will not let her fall.

This lesson is critical for real relationships. Without trust, dark romance-inspired dynamics collapse. They risk becoming frightening or even harmful. With trust, however, those same dynamics transform into some of the most exhilarating experiences a couple can share. Trust is built through consistency, respect, and care. It is reinforced when you honor boundaries every time, when you listen to unspoken cues, when you make her feel valued beyond the bedroom. Each moment of care is a deposit in the bank of trust, and those deposits are what allow for bold withdrawals later. The more trust she feels, the more she will lean into the experience—knowing she is cherished beneath the intensity.

In this way, emotional depth is not a soft addition to dark romance play. It is the mechanism that makes it possible. Intimacy ensures that passion is not reckless, but reverent.

Beyond the Bedroom: Intimacy That Fuels Fantasy

Dark romance is not limited to heated scenes or bold encounters. Its magic flows from the undercurrent of connection that threads through every interaction. The hero protects her outside the bedroom, shows loyalty in his actions, and prioritizes her in moments of calm. These everyday gestures make the fiery moments possible, because they create a baseline of safety and devotion.

Real life mirrors this dynamic. Emotional intimacy in daily life— listening to her frustrations, holding her hand, showing appreciation— builds the foundation. When a woman feels cared for in ordinary moments, she is far more likely to embrace extraordinary fantasies. Small acts of tenderness fuel the fire for darker explorations later.

Think of it as a balance: the shadows are thrilling only because the light of everyday intimacy shines behind them. Without the daily gestures of love, intensity feels hollow. With them, intensity feels profound. This is why men must cultivate emotional depth not only during intimacy but also in routine life. Every note of care, every act of presence, every word of reassurance strengthens the foundation. And that foundation makes fantasies not only possible, but unforgettable.

The Dark Romance Man's Advantage

At the heart of every dark romance story is a man who embodies both dominance and devotion. He is feared by others but trusted by her. He commands, but he also cherishes. He is strong, but he reveals just enough vulnerability to show that she alone holds the key to his soul.

For men in real life, this archetype offers a powerful lesson: emotional depth is the secret weapon. Strength alone may attract attention, but strength combined with intimacy creates lasting devotion. A man who learns to be present, to be vulnerable, to build trust, and to show care in daily life will find that dark romance fantasies do not remain confined to fiction. They come alive, because his partner feels safe enough to explore them and cherished enough to enjoy them fully.

Intimacy, then, is not a separate domain from passion. It is the force that elevates passion into something deeper. It is what makes intensity sustainable, fantasies fulfilling, and love unforgettable. The dark romance man who masters intimacy does more than fulfill desires—he becomes the desire.

CHAPTER 10 - THE DARK ROMANCE MAN'S CODE

"Power without restraint is tyranny. Restraint without passion is emptiness. The Dark Romance Man balances both."

Why a Code Matters

In fiction, the Dark Romance hero is larger than life. He's feared, desired, and unforgettable. But what makes him magnetic isn't chaos — it's his code. Women are drawn to men who are consistent in their power, passion, and purpose.

This code doesn't mean acting like a villain. It means embodying qualities that communicate strength, desire, and devotion while maintaining safety and respect.

Presence

Command Presence

- What It Means: The ability to lead without hesitation. In novels, the heroine is captivated not because he's reckless, but because he knows what he wants and takes it.

- Why It Works: Women equate decisiveness with security. When a man takes charge, he makes her feel both wanted and safe.
- How To Apply: Be clear in your words and actions. "Come here." "Look at me." These phrases project authority without cruelty.

Devotion

Fierce Devotion

- What It Means: Beneath the edge lies obsession. Heroes like Zade (Haunting Adeline) or Kai (Corrupt) terrify others, but for the heroine they're unwavering loyal.
- Why It Works: Devotion transforms intensity from selfishness into intimacy. She isn't just one option — she's the option.
- How To Apply: Express singular focus. Tell her: "You're the only one I want." Back it with action — protect her, prioritize her, and reassure her that she is the center of your world.

Danger

Controlled Danger

- What It Means: The Dark Romance Man flirts with danger but never loses control. He may be feared by others, but with her, his danger is always harnessed.
- Why It Works: Danger without control is terrifying. Danger under control is exhilarating. She feels the thrill without the risk.
- How To Apply: Use elements of edge — a firm grip, a whispered command — but pair them with boundaries. Let her know she can stop you anytime. This balance is what transforms fear into excitement.

Protection

Protective Instinct

- What It Means: The hero guards what's his. Not in a casual sense, but fiercely. In Butcher & Blackbird, this protection is raw, obsessive, almost primal.
- Why It Works: Protection signals safety. Even in the darkest scenarios, the heroine knows: he would never let real harm come to me.
- How To Apply: Pay attention to her comfort. Step in when she feels vulnerable. Create environments where she can explore fantasies without fear.

Honesty

Ruthless Honesty

- What It Means: The Dark Romance hero doesn't sugarcoat. He speaks truths others avoid. This raw honesty makes his devotion more believable.
- Why It Works: Brutal honesty cuts through doubt. When he says he wants her, she believes it — because he never lies.
- How To Apply: Tell her what you want, what you need, what you crave. Admit when you're vulnerable. Honesty builds intensity and trust.

Obsession

Ritual and Obsession

- What It Means: Small acts that show fixation — the way he touches her hair, repeats phrases, or marks her as his.

- Why It Works: Obsession feels intoxicating. To be the center of someone's ritual is to feel irreplaceable.
- How To Apply: Create your own rituals — a signature kiss, a phrase you whisper only to her. These become symbolic anchors of intimacy.

Sidebar – Why This Code Works

Psychologically, women crave certainty in intimacy. The Dark Romance Man's Code delivers certainty through contradictions:

- He is dangerous to others, safe for her.
- He is commanding, but devoted.
- He is honest, but tender.
- He is obsessed, but protective.

These contradictions make him larger than life — and unforgettable.

Reader Voices

"When he says, 'You're mine,' and proves it every day, I believe it with my whole body."

"The best thing isn't the danger — it's knowing I'm safe with him even in the middle of it."

"His honesty is brutal, but it makes me trust him more than anyone else."

Closing Thought

The Dark Romance Man isn't about cruelty or recklessness. He's about mastery — of himself, his partner, and the energy between them.

When men embrace this code, they don't just copy fictional heroes. They embody what those heroes symbolize: strength with restraint, passion with purpose, danger balanced by devotion.

Power without restraint is tyranny. Restraint without passion is emptiness. The Dark Romance Man balances both.

CHAPTER 11 - TURNING FANTASY INTO REALITY

"Fantasy becomes unforgettable when imagination is given breath, voice, and touch."

Why This Chapter Matters

Dark romance isn't merely a book category—it's a language of intensity. It speaks to the longing many women have to feel chosen with an edge, protected with force, and worshiped with undeniable certainty. The appeal is not just the plot twists; it's the sensation of being swept into a world where boundaries are clear, emotions run hot, and devotion feels absolute.

Yet stories live safely on the page. Real life needs care, structure, and responsibility so passion doesn't become panic. Turning fantasy into reality is about engineering intensity—building the container that lets both of you lean into bolder desires while staying unquestionably safe. Done well, these scenes can deepen trust, sharpen attraction, and create memories you'll both replay for years.

This chapter gives you twelve fully developed scenarios—complete with tone, dialogue, and step-by-step actions. Use them as scripts or inspiration. Swap words, adjust pacing, and tailor the energy to your partner. Your aim isn't theatrical perfection; it's presence. Speak clearly. Move with purpose. Watch her breathing, eyes, and posture. Every scene should feel like a daring duet where both of you know the steps.

The Framework

1. Consent First (Pre-Negotiation). Agree on themes that excite her, firm boundaries, and a safe word (e.g., "Yellow" for slow down, "Red" for stop). Decide what's off-limits, what's optional, and what's a green light.
2. Safety Next. Keep tools soft and skin-friendly. Avoid knots that tighten. Mind jewelry, hair, and circulation. Discuss where marks are okay (if at all).
3. Intensity with Balance. Pair every command with care: a rough grip followed by a palm to the cheek; a growl followed by a kiss to the forehead.
4. Check-Ins. In scene, use short questions: "Color?" "With me?" "Want more?" Outside scene, debrief honestly.
5. Aftercare Always. Blankets, water, cuddling, affirming words. Let adrenaline settle into tenderness.

Pro tip: Print or save these scripts. Highlight lines you love. Practice your tone—steady, low, deliberate.

1) The Captive and the Keeper

- **Set-Up**: Dim lights. Soft music. A silk scarf or wide ribbon. Guide her to sit on the edge of the bed or a chair. Make eye contact and say, "Color check?" When she gives the go-ahead, gently bind her wrists in front (not behind) and test for comfort.

- **Script & Actions**: Step close; let your breath warm her ear. "Tonight, you're mine. You stay where I put you." Stand back for a heartbeat—let anticipation bloom. Circle her slowly, fingertips skimming her shoulders and down her arms. Lift her chin with your knuckles. "Look at me." Hold her gaze; then deny a kiss by stopping a hair's breadth away. Run the silk along her collarbone; trace down the center of her chest; pause whenever her breath hitches. Move behind and anchor a firm palm on her sternum while your other hand steadies her thigh. "Good girl. Still."
- **Pleasure Focus**: Restriction amplifies sensation; every touch is brighter when she can't reach back.
- **Aftercare**: Untie carefully. Kiss any faint marks. Pull her onto your chest. "You did perfectly. I'm proud of you." Water, warmth, and a long hold.

2) The Masquerade Encounter

- **Set-Up**: A simple black mask (yours), her blindfold, lowered lights, and a single scented candle. Tell her: "When the mask is on, mystery rules." Safe word remains.
- **Script & Actions**: Approach without speaking. Let the mattress dip as you sit behind her. Tie the blindfold; check comfort. In a hushed voice: "You don't know who's touching you, but your body will answer me." Glide one fingertip along her wrist to elbow, then stop. Wait. Let silence press. Exhale at her neck; brush hair aside. "Say 'Please' if you want more." When she asks, reward with a slow, deliberate kiss on the shoulder. Alternate gentle strokes with firmer holds. Keep your voice low, a little distant: "You'll follow my voice… and only my voice."
- **Pleasure Focus**: Sensory deprivation heightens every sound and

touch; anticipation becomes electricity.

- **Aftercare**: Remove the blindfold slowly. Hold her face in both hands. "It was me the whole time. You're safe. You're adored."

3) The Forbidden Protector

- **Set-Up**: Choose a light role (professor, boss, bodyguard). Agree on boundaries—no humiliation, only confident guidance and praise-heavy dominance.
- **Script & Actions**: Square your shoulders; change your stance. "You didn't follow the rules." Pause. "Look at me." Let silence work. "You'll do as I say or face the consequences... understood?" Guide her to stand. Adjust her posture: a hand at her lower back, a fingertip lifting her chin. "Better. Now ask for what you want—clearly." When she does, reward with closeness: your palm spreads at her waist; your mouth lingers at the corner of hers without giving the full kiss. "That's my girl. Obey, and you get everything."
- **Pleasure Focus**: The thrill of authority safely held by someone trustworthy.
- **Aftercare**: Drop the role explicitly. "Scene off." Smile, soften. "Thank you for trusting me."

4) The Stalker's Shadow (Fantasy with Care)

- **Set-Up:** Only attempt with explicit pre-consent. Send two teasing texts earlier: "I saw you today." "I'll collect what's mine tonight." Agree on time and space; no actual lurking.
- **Script & Actions**: At home, dim lights. Approach from behind with deliberate footsteps so she hears you. Place a firm hand at her hip; the other covers her hand. Voice a whisper-rasp: "I've been watching you. Counting breaths. Tonight... you're mine." Turn her

gently to face you. Hold eye contact. Move slow, letting the tension stretch. Press her back to the wall with your forearm braced beside her head (never on her neck). "Tell me your color." When green, slide your palm from waist to jaw, thumb stroking once. "There she is." Tease with near-kisses; command small stillness: "Hands behind you. Good."

- **Pleasure Focus**: Curated obsession—desired, not dangerous.
- **Aftercare:** Name the fantasy to separate it from reality. "That was a role. In real life, you're safe, free, and fiercely loved."

5) The Dangerous Bargain

- **Set-Up**: Begin with a playful "debt" she "owes": a favor for a prior kindness or a bet she "lost." Keep it light, flirty, consensual.
- **Script & Actions:** Tap the invoice (imaginary) against your palm. "You owe me, and I always collect." Step closer. "Payment is obedience... for the next ten minutes." Set a timer if you like. "Stand here. Eyes on me." Give precise instructions: move a strand of her hair behind her ear, angle her hips, place her hands at her sides. Every compliance earns praise murmured at her skin. "Perfect. You learn quickly." Break tension with a slow, finally-given kiss. "Debt forgiven... for now."
- **Pleasure Focus:** Narrative inevitability—she's deliciously "trapped," yet fully safe.
- **Aftercare**: Light humor to re-ground. "Receipt paid in full." Cuddle and check feelings.

6) The Chase

- **Set-Up**: One room or two, soft rugs, no sharp corners. Agree on a "freeze" word (e.g., "Pause") if she wants you to stop immediately.

- **Script & Actions**: Start playful. "Run." Give her a two-second head start, then pursue with padded footsteps so she hears you coming. When you catch her, pin her gently to a wall or couch with your hips and an arm braced safely. Murmur at the corner of her mouth, barely touching: "You can't escape me." Let her try to wiggle free; relish the push-pull tension. Scoop her up; carry her three steps; set her down slowly to show control. "Caught you."
- **Pleasure Focus**: Adrenaline release turning into surrender.
- **Aftercare**: Laugh together, hydrate, breathe. "You were fast. I was faster." Long hug until heart rates calm.

7) The Ritual

- **Set-Up**: Candle, one signature song, and a phrase that will become "yours." Invite her into a small ceremony: phones off, door locked, deep breath together.
- **Script & Actions**: Face her, take both hands. "Tonight, you're mine in every way." Wait. "Say it back." When she repeats, kiss her knuckles. Place her hand over your heartbeat; place yours over hers. "One breath." Inhale together. Slowly guide her to kneel or sit at the bed's edge (pre-consented), crown her with your palm on her head for a second, then lift her chin. "I claim you. I care for you." Move with unhurried reverence—like each touch is a vow.
- **Pleasure Focus**: Ceremony re-frames intimacy as sacred and exclusive.
- **Aftercare**: End by repeating the phrase you began with. Forehead-to-forehead. "Ours alone."

8) The Rough Claim

- Set-Up: Pre-negotiate what kinds of roughness are okay (hair-pulling by the base, light spanking zones, intensity levels, no marks if needed). Have lotion or aloe nearby.

- Script & Actions: Close the distance abruptly; fist gently at the base of her hair and tilt her head, not jerking. Voice drops: "You're mine. Don't forget it." Press her to the mattress with a firm palm at the shoulder blade (never the neck). Alternate controlled swats with generous rubs and kisses. Count softly near her ear, "One... good girl," letting praise land after each surge. When she arches or gasps, slow down, check color, then resume with the pressure she prefers. Finish with a protective wrap of your body around hers.

- Pleasure Focus: Controlled intensity, endorphin lift, then melting release.

- Aftercare: Cool palms, slow kisses on any warmed skin, water, and soft blankets. "You're safe. I've got you."

9) The Silent Control

- Set-Up: Rule: no words from her; only nods, moans, or pointing to a prepared "need" card (water, slower, stop). You speak minimally.

- Script & Actions: Stand tall; gesture for her to come closer with two fingers. Place a finger lightly on her lips. "No words. Only what I pull from you." Guide her hand where you want it (on your chest, around your neck lightly—if pre-consented—on your shoulder). Watch her eyes. Reward compliance with measured touch; withdraw when she tries to speak to train the game's rhythm. Whisper: "Show me... don't tell me." When she obeys, murmur, "Yes. Just like that."

- Pleasure Focus: Quiet intensifies vulnerability and awareness; sensations get louder.

- Aftercare: Invite her voice back. "Tell me everything you felt." Listen fully, reassure, praise.

10) The Forbidden Public Touch

- Set-Up: Choose a public-but-innocent environment (restaurant booth, concert, a walk). No explicit acts, only suggestive closeness. Agree on signals and limits.
- Script & Actions: Sit beside her, not across. Let your knee brush hers; hold her hand under the table and stroke the inside of her wrist with your thumb. Lean in:
- "Smile. No one knows what I'm doing to you."
- Describe what you'll do later in her ear, slow and certain. Keep your face neutral when others look. Ask mundane questions in a steady voice while your hand is warm on her thigh (over clothing, respectful). "Be good, and I'll reward you when we're alone."
- Pleasure Focus: Secrecy, risk, composure—she glows knowing she's desired.
- Aftercare: Once private, praise her poise. "You were radiant." Offer water, decompress, transition into the next agreed scene—or simply cuddle.

11) The Protector's Shield

- **Set-Up**: Use a scenario where you "guard" her—storm outside, nightmare aftercare, or coming home from a stressful day. The tone is fierce devotion.
- **Script & Actions**: Pull her into your chest, broad and steady. "You're safe with me. Anyone who comes for you faces me first." Place a firm hand between her shoulder blades; the other cups the back of her head. Rock subtly. When she exhales, tip her chin and let your eyes say you mean it. "Give it to me—all the weight. I'll hold it." Transition into kisses that feel like shelter, not conquest. Keep your frame solid around her as she softens.

- **Pleasure Focus**: Trust and protection unlock surrender.
- **Aftercare**: Wrap in a blanket burrito. Tea or water. "I'm here all night. No rush, no demands."

12) The Obsessive Lover

- Set-Up: Agree that the language of "possession" is fantasy only. Decide which phrases excite and which are too much.
- Script & Actions: Step in close—closer than usual—and make your voice a vow.
- "You're mine. Not by force—by choice. I will not let you go."
- Trace her lower lip with your thumb, then deny the kiss. "Say it back." When she does, pace the repetition: "Again." Heat builds through claimed words. Hold her face in both hands and kiss her like you're sealing a promise. Between breaths: "Forever is a long time. I intend to spend it learning you."
- Pleasure Focus: The intoxication of being relentlessly wanted— held, not hunted.
- Aftercare: Re-anchor in reality. "You're free—and I choose you, again and again." Gentle laughter, shared breath, gratitude.

Closing Thought

Scenarios are invitations, not handcuffs. What makes them powerful isn't the prop or the exact sentence—it's your presence, your care, and your unwavering commitment to safety. When command is braided with devotion and play ends in tenderness, fantasy doesn't just imitate the stories she loves—it surpasses them, because it's yours.

CHAPTER 12 – FEMALE PERSPECTIVES:WHAT WOMEN WISH MEN UNDERSTOOD

"A woman may crave danger in fantasy, but in reality, what she wants most is a man she can trust to hold her through both the storm and the calm."

Introduction: Listening Beyond the Pages

Men often look at dark romance and ask, "Why this? Why him?" To many women, these stories aren't about cruelty or chaos; they're about longing, surrender, and the relief of being wanted beyond question. This chapter listens closely to women's voices—what draws them in, what they wish men understood, and how to translate the emotional electricity of fiction into real relationships rooted in trust and care.

The Allure of Darkness

Dark romance offers a safe way to explore taboo desires. The stakes feel dangerous, but the reader is safe on the couch, fully in control of the experience. That "protected risk" lets her ride waves of fear, thrill, arousal, and relief. Crucially, the darkness is usually paired with devotion and redemption: the hard, closed-off hero softens for one woman. She alone cracks his armor. That emotional victory—being chosen above all else—lands as deeply romantic. These heroines aren't weak. Even when outmatched, they show inner strength, boundaries, and moral gravity. Their influence reforms the hero. In effect, the story centers a woman's emotional perspective: her fear, desire, agency, and eventual power to be the one person who changes him.

Emotional Psychology and Desire

Women's desire tends to be highly contextual. Atmosphere, mood, trust, novelty, safety, and emotional connection are powerful accelerants. When a man's presence signals "you are safe, seen, and cherished," many women can let go more fully—ironically permitting darker, edgier play precisely because the foundation is solid. That's the secret many dark romances dramatize: the hero may be ruthless to the world, but he is unwavering devoted to her. He protects, prioritizes, and pursues with singular focus. That obsessive attention becomes its own kind of safety net. She feels special and secure enough to surrender.

Communication Gaps Men Miss

Partners often misread each other. Women may hint at fantasies, expecting a partner to pick up the vibe; men may be waiting for direct words. She might want more intensity but fears being judged. He might assume everything's fine because she hasn't asked for change. Bridging this gap is simple in principle: ask with curiosity, listen without judgment, and respond with care.

Dark romance can be a bridge. Discussing a scene or trope is less exposing than confessing raw desire. If she shares interest in a story line, hear it as an invitation, not a criticism. The message is: "I trust you with my imagination. Will you meet me there?"

Fantasy vs. Reality

Fantasies are not life plans. A woman can be turned on by a

ravishment scene in fiction yet want meticulous consent in real life. What many fantasies deliver is permission to surrender without guilt— she's wanted so completely that resistance melts. In reality, the container must be negotiated: clear limits, safe words, and enthusiastic consent. The point is never harm—it's the feeling of being overpowered by devotion, claimed by care, and held by a partner who is vigilant about her well-being.

What Women Wish Men Knew

- Emotional safety is sexy. Kindness, reliability, and steady attention don't "kill the spark"—they fuel it. When she trusts you, she'll go darker, deeper, and freer.
- Dominance isn't oppression. The draw isn't subjugation; it's leadership paired with tenderness. Take initiative, not control of her agency. Learn what dominance means to her—tone, pacing, commands, ritual—and build it together.
- Aftercare is half the scene. The storm is exciting; the anchor makes it unforgettable. Hold her, praise her, ground her, and check in the next day. That's how the fantasy becomes intimacy.
- Ask about her fantasies—and share yours. Treat them as creative blueprints, not demands. You're trying to capture a feeling (claimed, worshiped, overpowered, adored), not recreate a plot beat-for-beat.
- Consistency seduces. Grand gestures matter less than small, daily proofs that she's chosen. Follow-through is erotic.

Lessons from the Page (for Real Life)

Devotion as safety.

The anti-hero's "no one else but you" energy reassures. Translate that into everyday life with presence, exclusivity, and protection of her time and heart. Presence over performance. Slow your movements, lower your voice, hold her gaze. Create calm intensity. The aura matters as much as the act. Negotiation as foreplay.

Boundaries, safe words, and check-ins build anticipation. Planning a scene can feel like composing a symphony together. Vulnerability as power. When the "strong one" opens his soft underbelly just for her, the contrast hits like thunder. Share truth. It deepens everything.

Practical Applications

Read her cues: Breath, tension, stillness, eye contact—these are feedback. Ask softly: "More?" "Slower?" "Right there?"

Lead with clarity: Replace "What do you want to do?" with "Be ready at eight." Offer a container, not a commandment.

Build ritual: A text at noon, a certain song, a sentence that signals the switch ("You're mine tonight."). Shared language amplifies arousal.

Pair dark with tender: If you push, you also praise. If you bind, you also blanket. If you command, you also care. Review and refine. Afterward, debrief kindly: "What did you love? Anything to change?" Treat feedback as a gift.

Female Voices

"I don't want chaos. I want intensity wrapped in devotion."

"Make me the exception—dangerous to the world, gentle only for me."

"I'm not fragile. I want a man strong enough to hold all of me."

"If you create safety, I'll bring the storm."

Pulling It Together

Dark romance resonates because it captures a paradox women live comfortably with: ferocity and safety, surrender and choice, danger and devotion. The fantasy is a heightened version of what works in real life:

a man who leads with confidence, listens with care, and proves—again and again—that her heart is protected even when the scenes are not. When men understand this, the question shifts from "Why do women read these books?" to "How can I be the man who makes her feel that way?" The answer is not imitation, but integration: take the essence—devotion, intensity, leadership, tenderness—and weave it into your way of loving. If you do, you won't just admire the hero on the page. You'll become the one she dreams about—and reaches for—when the lights go down.

CHAPTER 13 – THE ART OF AFTERCARE

"Intensity without tenderness is cruelty. The scene is not complete until her body and heart are held, calmed, and cherished."

Introduction: Aftercare Is Not Optional

If there is one principle that separates a true Dark Romance Man from a pretender, it is this: aftercare is not optional. It is not a side note, not an extra, not a sweet add-on if you happen to remember. Aftercare is the heart of dark romance. It is mandatory. It is non-negotiable. Without it, all the passion, all the role-play, all the intensity collapses into selfishness or worse. With it, the intensity transforms into trust, intimacy, and lasting connection.

Think of aftercare as the moment when the storm gives way to the calm. The lightning and thunder are thrilling; they electrify the air. But when the storm passes, the world needs sunlight, stillness, and grounding. Without that calm, the storm leaves damage. Without aftercare, passion leaves wounds.

Too many men make the mistake of focusing only on the high-octane moments: the seduction, the role-play, the dominance, the sex itself. They forget that the most powerful impact on a woman is often what happens after. A man who knows how to dominate but does not know how to comfort, reassure, and ground his partner is incomplete. He has only learned half the art.

Aftercare is what cements trust. It is what makes her feel safe to surrender the next time. It is what transforms an edgy fantasy into a shared secret memory she treasures rather than regrets. And it is what allows her body and emotions to settle, to integrate the intensity, and to associate you with warmth, security, and love rather than chaos.

To skip aftercare is to betray the very essence of dark romance. The genre thrives on intensity, danger, and surrender, yes—but also on devotion, tenderness, and safety. A heroine who is ravished in one scene is always held in the next. A man who claims her body in a storm must also claim her heart in the quiet that follows.

Why Aftercare Matters So Deeply

1. Physiological reasons – During intense intimacy, adrenaline, dopamine, and Oxycontin flood her system. When the scene ends, her body can feel shaky, overstimulated, or even depleted. Aftercare soothes her nervous system. Physical touch, gentle words, and calm presence help her regulate.

2. Emotional reasons – Dark romance play often brushes against fear, vulnerability, or shame. Aftercare reminds her she is loved, valued, and safe. It tells her, "What just happened was play, not rejection or disrespect." This reassurance is vital.

3. Relational reasons – Aftercare deepens the bond. It is in these moments—when you hold her, stroke her hair, whisper affirmations—that she feels most profoundly connected to you. The intensity of the scene amplifies the tenderness of the aftermath.

Mandatory, Not Negotiable

Every man must engrave this truth into his behavior: aftercare is not a favor; it is a duty. A man who wants the privilege of leading a woman into intensity must also take full responsibility for guiding her safely back out of it.

You don't get to decide whether she "needs" aftercare. She does. And even if she insists she doesn't, offer it anyway. In time, she will come to expect it—and that is good. A woman who expects aftercare is a woman who knows her worth, and a man who provides it proves his.

Without aftercare, the scene is unfinished. The fantasy remains jagged, unresolved. With aftercare, the scene becomes complete, whole, unforgettable.

The Signal of a True Dark Romance Man

What distinguishes a Dark Romance Man is not how well he commands, but how well he cares. Any man can bark orders or try to play the alpha. Few men can pair strength with gentleness, danger with safety, intensity with tenderness. That is why women crave the archetype: not because he is brutal, but because he is brutal to the world and gentle to her.

Aftercare is the litmus test of that gentleness. It is where he proves that his dominance was never about ego, cruelty, or power for its own sake. It was about giving her an experience, fulfilling a fantasy, and then loving her back into wholeness afterward.

If you take nothing else from this book, take this: without aftercare, there is no dark romance.

CHAPTER 14 - BECOMING THE DARK ROMANCE MAN

"To claim her body, you must first captivate her mind."

The Foundation: Confidence Rooted in Presence

The Dark Romance Man doesn't mumble. He doesn't shuffle in the background. He is present. His strength comes not from arrogance but from an ability to own the room and make his partner feel like the center of it. Stand tall, maintain eye contact, and let silence work for you. Speak deliberately, as though every word is chosen for effect. When you touch, do it with intention, not hesitation.

Reader's Voice:

"When he looked at me across the table and didn't break eye contact, I felt my whole body respond. It was like being seen in a way I didn't know I needed."

Controlled Obsession

In novels, women swoon not because the man is casual, but because he is obsessed. He knows her scent, her expressions, her flaws — and treasures them. In reality, this doesn't mean unhealthy control; it means attentiveness so intense that she feels singular and irreplaceable. Practical examples include remembering details she shares, noticing small changes, and making her feel like there's no one else in the room when you speak to her.

Dominance Without Cruelty

Dominance is central to dark romance — but in reality, it thrives only when paired with consent, safety, and mutual excitement. Dominance here means leading with strength, creating structure, and guiding experiences.

Reader's Voice

"He didn't just take control; he made me feel like I could trust him with everything."

The Art of Mystery

The Dark Romance Man reveals himself in layers. He is not a loud over sharer. Instead, he keeps a part of himself hidden, drawing her deeper with every revelation. Share glimpses of your inner world without handing everything at once. Let actions speak louder than explanations. Use silence strategically — it creates curiosity.

Emotional Intensity

The archetype thrives on intensity — not just in the bedroom, but in every exchange. A dark romance hero doesn't make a compliment forgettable; he makes it a declaration. Replace plain remarks with declarations that capture obsession and devotion.

Rituals of Protection

A cornerstone of the Dark Romance Man is protection — not in the sense of fragility, but in creating an environment where she feels safe to let go. Check in often, provide aftercare habits like blankets or tea, and build a sense of safety that makes risk possible.

Scenarios in Practice

Becoming the Dark Romance Man is about practice, not theory. Three small, practical role-play scenarios:

a) The Slow Burn — maintain intense eye contact at dinner, whisper something leaving no doubt about your desire, make her wait for your touch until both are restless.

b) The Protector — guide her with a firm hand at the small of her back, pull her closer than necessary through a doorway.

c) The Command — at home, catch her gaze and say, "Tonight, you're mine," then follow through with intentional touches and clear leadership.

Mini-Takeaway

Becoming the Dark Romance Man isn't about acting like someone else. It's about amplifying qualities you already have — confidence, focus, intensity — and delivering them with deliberate presence. It's a role that demands both strength and tenderness, mystery and safety. The result is a man who feels larger than life, both in fantasy and in reality.

Consent, Safety, and Boundaries: The Core of Real Power

No matter how intense, dominant, or obsessive the Dark Romance Man may appear, his true strength lies in the respect he shows for his partner's safety and autonomy. In every scenario, fantasy, or role-play, consent is what transforms darkness into desire, and boundaries are what make surrender possible. To embody this archetype in reality means understanding that consent is not a one-time check — it is continuous, verbal and nonverbal, before, during, and after. Boundaries are not restrictions, but a framework that creates trust and heightens intensity. Safety does not dull passion; it intensifies it, because your partner can let go knowing you will catch her.

Reader's Voice:

"The most powerful moment wasn't when he took control — it was when I realized he was paying attention to every signal I gave, making me feel both consumed and completely safe."

Final Thought

Becoming the Dark Romance Man is not about fear, cruelty, or reckless abandon. It is about harnessing presence, mystery, and dominance while honoring her trust above all else. The paradox is that the darker the fantasy, the greater the need for light — and that light is built on respect.

CHAPTER 15 - THE CINEMATIC CLOSING

"A fantasy is not meant to stay on the page. It is meant to breathe between two lovers who dare to make it real."

Why an Ending Matters

Every great story has a climax — and so must your journey into the world of dark romance. The books women devour don't just end with heat; they end with intensity, obsession, and a sense that what just happened will change everything.

Your partner doesn't want a forgettable night. She wants moments so vivid they replay in her memory like scenes from her favorite novels. The Cinematic Closing is about ensuring that the way you finish intimacy leaves her trembling not only from pleasure, but from emotional aftershock.

Symbolism
  End with Symbolism

- In Fiction: Climaxes are marked by declarations, confessions, or gestures of obsession.
- In Real Life: Choose a signature act to end your encounters

—whispering the same phrase, marking her body with kisses, or holding her in a particular way.

- Why It Works: Symbols anchor memory. Repetition of an intense closing gesture conditions her to crave it.

Emotional
Make It Emotional, Not Just Physical

- In Fiction: Heroes often confess vulnerability in the aftermath of passion — "You're mine." "I can't lose you."
- In Real Life: After sex, speak from the heart. Say the words you might normally hold back.
- Why It Works: Post-orgasm, emotions are raw. A sincere confession in that moment lands deeper than at any other time.

Scene
Build a Scene She Can Replay

- In Fiction: Final moments are described with cinematic detail — the scent, the light, the exact look in his eyes.
- In Real Life: Create scenes with atmosphere. Light candles, keep the music playing, or use a certain touch that she can associate with "the end."
- Why It Works: Memories attach to sensory detail. The richer the scene, the more unforgettable it becomes.

Finale
The Dark Romance Man's Finale

Here are three ways to close like a hero from her favorite book:

- The Claim – Hold her face, stare into her eyes, and whisper: "You're mine. Forever."
- The Protector – Wrap her in your arms and say: "Nothing will ever touch you while I'm here."
- The Worshiper – Kiss her body slowly, whispering: "You're everything I've ever wanted."

Each finale blends dominance, devotion, and emotional vulnerability — the trifecta of the Dark Romance man.

Sidebar – Why Women Remember Endings

Psychologists call it the "peak-end rule." People remember two moments most: the peak of intensity and the end of the experience. If you want her to replay your time together like her favorite scene, you must master both.

Reader Voices

"It wasn't the sex I remembered — it was the way he held me after like he couldn't let go."

"When he whispered that I belonged to him, I felt it in my bones."

"The closing moment is what makes me crave the next time."

Closing Thought

This book began with an introduction to dark romance, and it ends with a challenge: don't just read about fantasy — become it.

The Cinematic Closing is your final chance to embody the Dark Romance hero: commanding yet tender, dangerous yet safe, obsessive yet protective. When you finish with devotion and drama, you don't just end the night — you create a memory she will carry forever.

"A fantasy is not meant to stay on the page. It is meant to breathe between two lovers who dare to make it real."

APPENDICES

"Fantasy is not only lived in the moment — it is built before, heightened during, and nurtured after."

Why These Appendices Exist

Throughout this book, you've learned the foundations of what makes dark romance compelling: intensity, fantasy, desire, and the delicate balance of safety and surrender, but theory alone isn't enough. These appendices were created to give you practical tool
— the actual words, prompts, and actions you can use in real situations.

A common challenge men face is not a lack of willingness, but a lack of language and structure. Many men know they want to create excitement and intimacy, but they don't know what to say or how to begin. These lists are designed to bridge that gap, offering ready-made phrases, scene starters, and aftercare reminders so that you can move with confidence.

How to Use These Tools

- Think of the appendices as a toolkit. Not every phrase or prompt will fit your personality, nor should you try to use them all. Instead:
- Select what feels authentic — choose phrases or prompts that

naturally align with your energy and your partner's desires.

- Adapt as needed — rephrase in your own words while keeping the same energy.
- Introduce gradually — try one or two at a time rather than overwhelming the moment.
- Always center consent and comfort — even the darkest lines work best when your partner feels safe, desired, and respected.
- When used with intention, these tools stop being "lines from a book" and instead become part of your natural behavior.

The Four Appendices

Appendix A: 100 Weighted Phrases for Connection and Anticipation
Emotional anchors designed to strengthen your bond, build suspense, and heighten her
sense of being chosen.

Appendix B: 100 Scene Starters and Prompts

A collection of short, role-play cues and atmospheric lines. These set the stage for
fantasy-driven encounters, build tension, and make it easy for you to create the
cinematic mood of dark romance.

Appendix C: 100 Intimacy Phrases

A library of phrases that capture the tone of dark romance during intimate moments —
from dominance to tenderness.

Appendix D: 100 Aftercare Actions and Phrases

Guidance for what comes after passion. These phrases and actions ensure your partner

feels secure, valued, and cared for, turning intensity into lasting intimacy.

Closing Reflection

Becoming a Dark Romance Man is not about memorizing lines or mimicking fiction. It's about behavior, execution, and presence.

The tools in these appendices will help you:

- Speak with boldness when confidence matters.
- Show care when aftercare is needed.
- Build anticipation and tension that makes her heart race.
- Create scenarios that feel cinematic, unforgettable, and deeply personal.

Use these words and prompts as stepping stones, not crutches. Over time, they will blend with your own voice until they feel natural. When you combine them with empathy, attentiveness, and respect, you will embody the essence of the Dark Romance Man — a man who makes his partner feel desired, safe, and fully alive.

APPENDIX I - PHRASES FOR ANTICIPATION, INTENSITY, AND BONDING

"Words are not filler; they are fire. Each one builds the world she lives in with you."

This appendix is not about what you say in the heat of intimacy — that is covered elsewhere. Instead, these 100 weighted phrases are designed to build anticipation, deepen emotional connection, and create an atmosphere of intensity long before clothes ever come off.

Dark romance thrives on tension: the stolen glance, the obsessive confession, the whispered promise of something yet to come. When spoken with conviction, these lines serve three key purposes:
1. They build anticipation.
2. They increase emotional weight.
3. They strengthen the bond.

The goal is not to memorize them like a script but to let them inspire your own words. Delivered at the right moment, they can change the air between you, making her feel wanted, seen, and desired.

Everyday Affection
   "I love how you make the room brighter just by being in it."

"You make me want to be the best version of myself."

"I never get tired of hearing your laugh."

"You make ordinary days feel extraordinary."

"I love the way your eyes light up when you smile."

"Being with you is the best part of my day."

"You make me feel at home, no matter where we are."

"I admire how strong and graceful you are."

"You're the first person I want to tell my good news to."

"Holding you feels like peace."

"You make even silence feel comforting."

"I'm grateful for you every single day."

"You are the calm to my storms."

"You make life feel richer."

"I could listen to your stories forever."

"You make me believe in better days."

"I admire how thoughtful you are."

"You make simple moments special."

"Being with you feels effortless."

"I love how you always understand me."

Building Anticipation

"I've been thinking about you all day."

"I can't wait to get you alone later."

"You have no idea what you do to me."

"I'm counting down the minutes until I see you."

"I can still feel your touch from last night."

"Just hearing your voice drives me wild."

"I'm already imagining how good you'll feel in my arms."

"The way you looked at me earlier has me restless."

"I love how you keep me craving more."

"Every time I see you, I want you even more."

"You don't even realize how tempting you are."
"I love watching you when you think I'm not looking."
"I keep replaying our last kiss in my head."
"You have me distracted in the best way."
"The thought of you keeps me awake at night."
"You leave me wanting more every time."
"I can't stop imagining what I'll do to you later."
"You've been on my mind nonstop."
"You know how much I crave you, don't you?"
"Just one touch from you is enough to unravel me."

Deep Connection
"You're the only person I can truly open up to."
"I trust you with every part of me."
"Being with you feels like home."
"I love how you always know what I'm thinking."
"You see the best in me when I can't."
"I feel safe when I'm with you."
"I love how we can talk about anything."
"You make me feel understood."
"I'm proud to share my life with you."
"You're my favorite person in the world."
"I feel complete when I'm with you."
"You make me want to open up more."
"I admire how deeply you care for me."
"You know me better than anyone else."
"I love how you always listen without judgment."
"You inspire me to be vulnerable."
"I feel like I can be my true self around you."
"You make me want to share my secrets."
"I never feel alone when I'm with you."

"Loving you feels natural."

Encouragement and Support

"I believe in you no matter what."

"You inspire me every single day."

"You're stronger than you realize."

"I know you can handle anything."

"I'm so proud of everything you do."

"You amaze me with your determination."

"You're capable of anything you set your mind to."

"I admire how you never give up."

"You're more resilient than you think."

"I trust your decisions completely."

"I know you'll achieve your dreams."

"You handle challenges with such grace."

"I admire your courage."

"You make me want to push harder too."

"I'll always be here to support you."

"You inspire me to grow."

"You're unstoppable."

"I love your drive and ambition."

"I'm proud to stand by your side."

"You make me admire strength in new ways."

Romantic Intensity

"You make my heart race."

"I crave you every second we're apart."

"I want to memorize every inch of you."

"You're the most intoxicating person I've ever met."

"You set my soul on fire."

"I'm addicted to the way you make me feel."

"No one has ever had this effect on me."

"I want you more than I've ever wanted anything."

"You make everything else fade away."

"I can't get enough of you."

"You make desire feel endless."

"Being near you is electrifying."

"You take my breath away."

"Every kiss feels like the first time."

"I lose myself when I'm with you."

"You're my favorite kind of chaos."

"You make love feel dangerous and safe at once."

"You've ruined me for anyone else."

"I want you, always."

"I burn for you."

APPENDIX II - STARTERS AND PROMPTS

This appendix offers a curated list of 100 quick scene starters — short, atmospheric lines and prompts you can use to ignite role-play, spark anticipation, and set the tone for dark romance encounters. They are designed to be direct, simple to use, and adaptable to different settings. Use them sparingly, with awareness of your partner's comfort and consent, and they will transform the ordinary into something unforgettable.

Dominance & Control
"Don't move until I say."
"Look at me when I speak."
"On your knees, right here."
"You're mine tonight."
"Keep your eyes closed until I tell you."
"Hands behind your back."
"Crawl to me slowly."
"Don't speak unless I ask you a question."
"Give me your wrists."
"Wait for me in the dark."
"Stay perfectly still."
"Do not touch me until I allow it."
"Whisper my name."

"Count every second until I return."

"Obey, and I'll reward you."

"Don't you dare move."

"Hold your breath."

"I'll tell you when you've had enough."

"You will do as I say."

"Kneel, and don't break eye contact."

Atmospheric & Mysterious

"The lights stay off."

"Listen to the sound of my footsteps."

"Don't turn around."

"Imagine me watching you."

"Feel the silence between us."

"Pretend you don't know what happens next."

"I'll find you, no matter where you hide."

"Tonight, nothing else exists but this."

"You don't see me, but I see everything."

"Let the darkness guide you."

"Picture my hands before they touch you."

"Forget the world outside this room."

"This moment belongs only to us."

"You can't escape me."

"The air is heavy with what's coming."

"Do you feel the tension building?"

"Every shadow in here belongs to me."

"Don't ask questions — surrender to the unknown."

"Imagine I'm already behind you."

"Trust me enough to let go."

Teasing & Anticipation

"You'll beg before I'm done."

"I'll stop if you ask — but you won't."

"You have no idea what's coming."

"The more you resist, the more I'll enjoy this"

"You think you can handle me?"

"I'll make you crave more than you can stand."

"You won't sleep after tonight."

"I know exactly how to unravel you."

"Say my name like you need me."

"Every second makes you weaker."

"You're not ready for what I'm about to do."

"I'll make you forget your own name."

"You'll ache for me when it's over."

"Try to hide your desire — I'll see it anyway."

"You think you can outlast me?"

"I'll prove you wrong."

"The more you wait, the sweeter it gets."

"You're already trembling, aren't you?"

"I'll draw this out until you can't take it."

"You're not in control anymore."

Romantic Darkness

"You are the only light I want."

"I'd burn the world before I'd lose you."

"No one else will ever have you."

"You belong only to me."

"I'll guard you even from yourself."

"You are mine to protect and to ruin."

"I crave every part of you — even the parts you hide."

"You'll never doubt how much I need you."

"Even your fears are beautiful to me."

"I'll always catch you, no matter how far you fall."
"You are my addiction."
"Nothing will take you from me."
"You're worth every shadow I carry."
"My obsession is your devotion."
"Every scar of mine belongs to you now."
"I'd destroy everything for one more night with you."
"You'll never escape my desire."
"You are my ruin, and I welcome it."
"I want every piece of your darkness."
"You make me dangerous, and I don't care."

Scene-Setting Prompts
"Meet me blindfolded."
"Knock three times before you enter."
"Wait in silence until I arrive."
"Wear what I tell you, nothing else."
"Leave the door unlocked for me."
"Sit on the edge of the bed and wait."
"Light only one candle."
"Let the music play until I say stop."
"Stand by the window and don't move."
"Wait for my touch in total darkness."
"Write down your deepest secret and hand it to me."
"Stand barefoot and close your eyes."
"Don't turn around when I approach."
"Be ready when I call your name."
"Leave the phone on — I want to hear you."
"Sit in my chair until I take it back."
"Count backwards until I interrupt you."
"Lock the world out — only us tonight."

"Don't prepare — just obey."

"Wait. I'm coming for you."

APPENDIX III - DARK ROMANCE PHRASES FOR INTIMATE MOMENTS

"Sometimes the right words can unlock the deepest surrender."

This appendix provides a curated list of 100 phrases a man can say during intimacy to echo the intensity, obsession, and emotional weight found in dark romance novels.

These aren't just lines — they are tools. When spoken with confidence and conviction, they transform a moment from ordinary to unforgettable.

Possession & Obsession
  "You're mine. Always."
  "Every inch of you belongs to me."
  "No one else will ever have you."
  "Say you're mine."
  "I can't get enough of you. I never will."
  "Even if you run, I'll find you."
  "Your body remembers me, even when your mind resists."
  "No one touches you but me."

"I'd burn the world before I'd lose you."

"You're my addiction."

"Every breath you take is mine."

"You can fight me, but I'll still win you."

"You'll never escape me."

"You belong to me more than you belong to yourself."

"I'd kill for you. I'd die for you."

"I don't want you to love me—I want you to need me."

"You're my obsession, my madness, my salvation."

"Your surrender is the only thing I crave."

"I'll haunt you until the end of time."

"You were made for me."

Command & Control

"Look at me when I touch you."

"Hands above your head."

"Don't move until I say."

"Beg for me."

"Open your mouth."

"You take what I give you, nothing more."

"Kneel."

"You obey me, and you love it."

"Hold still. Let me enjoy this."

"Don't speak unless I allow it."

"Spread for me."

"Stay quiet, or I'll make you scream louder."

"On your knees."

"Show me how much you want me."

"Wait. I'm not finished with you yet."

"Keep your eyes on me."

"Say my name. Louder."

"I decide when this ends."

"Submit to me."

"Do exactly as I say, and I'll reward you."

Danger & Edge Play

"You should run. But you won't."

"You're trembling, and it excites me."

"Scream if you want—no one will hear you but me."

"I could break you. But I won't. Not tonight."

"You like being scared, don't you?"

"The darker it gets, the more you want me."

"You should be afraid right now. But you're not, are you?"

"I'll ruin you—and you'll beg me for more."

"You don't get to escape."

"The danger makes you wet."

"You crave the monster in me."

"Your fear tastes like desire."

"I could devour you whole."

"You're playing with fire, and you love the burn."

"I'll take you in the dark, where no one else can see."

"The thrill is knowing I might go too far."

"You wanted danger—now you've found it."

"If I let go, you'd be lost. Forever."

"You'll remember this every time you close your eyes."

"You don't survive me. You surrender to me".

Praise & Worship

"You're perfect when you obey."

"No one else could take me like you do."

"You make me lose control."

"No one has ever undone me like this."

"You're the only one who could break me."

"Every sound you make drives me insane."

"Your body was made for mine."

"You're my goddess, my ruin."

"I've never wanted anyone like this."

"The way you beg makes me harder."

"You're the reason I can't stop."

"You feel better than sin."

"Every moan is my victory."

"You don't even know how irresistible you are."

"You're all I think about."

"You drive me mad with desire."

"You're everything I never knew I needed."

"No one compares to you. No one."

"You're heaven wrapped in temptation."

"I'd worship you for eternity."

Promises & Forever

"Even death couldn't keep me from you."

"You're not just my now—you're my always."

"I'll love you until my last breath—and beyond."

"Even if the world ends, I'll still crave you."

"I'd choose you in every lifetime."

"No matter where you go, I'll follow."

"You're the only forever I want."

"My soul is yours."

"I'll never stop hunting for you."

"Every life I live, it will always be you."

"You'll never be rid of me."

"I'm bound to you, body and soul."

"We're inevitable."

"Nothing will tear us apart—not heaven, not hell."

"I'll want you when we're old. When we're ashes. Always."

"If I die, I'll come back just to find you."

"Forever isn't long enough for me with you."

"Even my ghosts will belong to you."

"There's no end to us. Not ever."

"You are my eternity."

APPENDIX IV - AFTERCARE PHRASES, BEHAVIORS, AND ACTIVITIES

"Intensity means nothing without tenderness after."

Dark romance thrives on extremes — danger and safety, dominance and surrender, intensity and softness. Aftercare is where those extremes are balanced and trust is reinforced.

This appendix offers 100 examples of aftercare: things you can say, do, or provide after an intimate scene or role play.

Verbal Reassurance (Phrases) - Words spoken in a soft, steady tone to affirm love, safety, and devotion.
  "You're safe with me."
  "I love you more than you'll ever know."
  "Thank you for trusting me."
  "You did so perfectly for me."
  "I'm so proud of you."
  "You're everything I want."
  "I'll never hurt you outside of what we choose together."
  "I adore you."

"You're my whole world."

"I've got you. Always."

"Did I go too far? Tell me everything."

"I hear you. I see you."

"You're more precious to me than anything."

"I'm right here. I'm not going anywhere."

"You're so beautiful to me."

"I need you as much as you need me."

"I love the way you trust me."

"You make me better."

"I'll hold you as long as you need."

"You're safe, you're mine, you're loved."

"I wouldn't change a single thing about you."

"Thank you for letting me have all of you."

"You're everything I never knew I needed."

"I love you beyond words."

"Rest now. I've got you."

Physical Comfort (Behaviors) - Simple, grounding actions that reestablish safety through touch.

- Hold her tightly against your chest until her breathing steadies.
- Wrap your arms around her from behind and rock her gently.
- Stroke her hair slowly.
- Kiss her forehead softly.
- Rub slow circles on her back.
- Keep a hand on her thigh or waist for constant reassurance.
- Pull the blankets over both of you.
- Rest your forehead against hers and breathe together.
- Brush her cheek with your thumb.
- Massage her scalp while she rests on your chest.
- Pull her into your lap and cradle her.

- Wrap her completely in your arms and whisper reassurance.
- Play with her fingers gently, weaving them with yours.
- Stroke her arm or leg in slow, steady lines.
- Press a lingering kiss on her temple.
- Keep your body touching hers until she falls asleep.
- Cuddle in silence.
- Rock her slowly as if swaying to a song.
- Rest your hand over her heart so she feels your warmth.
- Tuck her hair behind her ear and smile at her.

Acts of Care (Activities) - Showing love through actions that meet her needs after intensity.

- Bring her a glass of water.
- Offer her a warm blanket.
- Run a bath for her.
- Get her favorite snack or chocolate.
- Make her tea.
- Adjust the pillows so she's comfortable.
- Fetch her a hoodie or shirt of yours to wear.
- Help her into bed gently.
- Wipe her down with a warm cloth.
- Order food for her if she's hungry.
- Light a candle to soften the room's mood.
- Play quiet, soothing music.
- Turn on a fan or adjust the room's temperature.
- Lay beside her silently until she speaks.
- Offer her your chest as a pillow.
- Rub lotion on her hands or feet.
- Clean up the space quickly so she feels cared for.

- Warm her socks or blanket in the dryer.
- Whisper: "Stay here. I'll handle everything."
- Sit by her side, brushing her skin lightly while she rests.

Connection Rituals - Ways to deepen intimacy and ensure emotional grounding.

- Ask her: "What part did you love most?"
- Share: "My favorite moment was when you..."
- Look into her eyes silently for a full minute.
- Hold hands tightly until she squeezes back.
- Repeat a ritual phrase: "We're back. We're safe."
- Make her laugh with a gentle joke to release tension.
- Remind her of a private nickname.
- Ask: "Do you need me softer now?"
- Talk about something light, like tomorrow's plans.
- Whisper what you adore about her body.
- Ask if she wants to be held tighter or looser.
- Give her space if she asks, but stay nearby.
- Listen if she wants to talk about how she felt.
- Share how much you loved her trust.
- Kiss her hand as a gesture of reverence.
- Create a ritual touch—like pressing foreheads together to "return."
- Tell her one thing you learned about her tonight.
- End the night with: "You're my forever."
- Repeat: "We're okay. We're better than okay."
- Remind her: "No one else will ever have this with me."

Playful Softness - Gentle, lighthearted gestures that break tension and bring warmth.

- Tickle her lightly until she giggles.
- Make a silly face after a kiss.
- Whisper: "You're adorable when you blush."
- Blow on her neck playfully.
- Call her by a goofy pet name only you use.
- Tell her she's trouble—but smile when you say it.
- Wrap her up in a "blanket burrito."
- Put on her favorite song and dance clumsily with her.
- Pretend to "lock" her in your arms.
- Murmur: "I'd still choose you, even if you were chaos."
- Brush her nose with yours.
- Tell her: "You're the best bad idea I've ever had."
- Nuzzle into her neck and refuse to move.
- Whisper: "Let's never leave this bed."
- End with: "You're safe, you're mine, you're loved."

The "Her Darkest Desires" Series by S.D. Ossessione

Continue your journey with other books in the **Her Darkest Desires** series by S.D. Ossessione. Each volume draws you further into the shadows of passion and power, where intimacy becomes daring, and desire transforms into obsession. Within these pages you will find whispered secrets, dangerous temptations, and the kind of unforgettable intimacy that lingers long after the night ends.

Collect every volume to explore new fantasies, unlock deeper desires, and discover how passion becomes obsession, and how obsession becomes the bond that ties lovers closer than ever before.

About the Author

S.D. Ossessione writes not from theory, but from lived experience. As an individual partnered with someone who has a deep love for dark romance novels, I have had the unique opportunity to explore how fantasy and fiction can overflow into real intimacy. What began as simple curiosity—listening to the stories and tropes that stirred her imagination—soon grew into a shared passion, where literature inspired experimentation, and fantasy became a tool for deepening our bond.

Through trial, error, and discovery, we found that these novels offer more than entertainment; they carry powerful lessons about communication, trust, and desire. The result was not only greater passion, but a stronger connection. Out of this journey came the understanding that dark romance, when translated carefully into real-life intimacy, requires more than role-play. It requires respect, aftercare, self-awareness, and the courage to both lead and be vulnerable.

This book is the culmination of that exploration. It shares the essential do's and don't s, the insights gained from our own experiences, and the strategies that any man can use to unlock this world for himself and his partner. My hope is that readers—whether seasoned romantics or hesitant newcomers—find practical guidance, inspiration, and confidence to step into these roles in a way that is authentic, safe, and deeply satisfying.

At its heart, this work is an invitation: to learn, to explore, and to enjoy the mysterious and thrilling world of dark romance—not just on the page, but in the intimacy of real life.